GETTING STARTED WITH IMOVIE

AN INSANELY EASY GUIDE TO MOVIE EDITING WITH IMOVIE

SCOTT LA COUNTE

RIDICULOUSLY SIMPLE BOOKS

ANAHEIM, CALIFORNIA

www.RidiculouslySimpleBooks.com

Copyright © 2022 by Scott La Counte.

All rights reserved. No part of this publication may be reproduced, distributed or transmitted in any form or by any means, including photocopying, recording, or other electronic or mechanical methods, without the prior written permission of the publisher, except in the case of brief quotations embodied in critical reviews and certain other noncommercial uses permitted by copyright law.

Limited Liability / Disclaimer of Warranty. While best efforts have been used in preparing this book, the author and publishers make no representations or warranties of any kind and assume no liabilities of any kind with respect to accuracy or completeness of the content and specifically the author nor publisher shall be held liable or responsible to any person or entity with respect to any loss or incidental or consequential damages caused or alleged to have been caused, directly, or indirectly without limitations, by the information or programs contained herein. Furthermore, readers should be aware that the Internet sites listed in this work may have changed or disappeared. This work is sold with the understanding that the advice inside may not be suitable in every situation.

Trademarks. Where trademarks are used in this book, this infers no endorsement or any affiliation with this book. Any trademarks (including, but not limiting to, screenshots) used in this book are solely used for editorial and educational purposes.

Disclaimer: Please note, while every effort has been made to ensure accuracy, this book is not endorsed by Apple, Inc. and should be considered unofficial.

Table of Contents

INTRODUCTION **6**

START HERE **7**
    iMovie for… 7
    Let's Get Started! 8

MAGIC MOVIE MODE **13**
    Magic Moments In Seconds 13
    Creating An Album 13
    Making the Magical Moments 18
    Sharing and Playing Video 30
    Moving Video From iPhone / iPad to Mac 32

STORYBOARDS MODE **35**
    Editing a Storyboard 44

MAKE A MOVIE FROM SCRATCH **47**
    Manual Controls *51*
    Adding Transitions *53*

IMOVIE FOR MACOS **54**
    Downloading iMovie *54*
    Starting a New Project *55*
    Creating Your First Movie *57*
    Creating Title, Backgrounds, Transitions, and More *59*
    Managing the Film Editor *59*
    Editing Clips *60*
    Editing a Clip *65*
    Add a Voiceover *66*
    Add a Theme *67*
    Saving / Sharing Movie *68*

INDEX **69**

ABOUT THE AUTHOR **71**

INTRODUCTION

While taking impressive photos may be on many people's minds when they first turn on their iPhones and iPads, the video capability is so good, it's used by professional cinematographers.

But recording video, and then turning it into a movie that feels cinematic are two different things. Yes, you can easily take videos and watch them—but what about editing them? What about adding cool effects to them? What about splicing in other videos?

With Apple, things just kind of work. They have a brilliant way of making things that used to be complicated…simple. This is especially true with Apple's iMovie software.

This book will walk you through what you need to know to create gorgeous videos that you can share with family and friends. Some of the things you'll discover inside:

- Using Magic Movie
- Designing your movie with Storyboard
- Using Cinematic mode
- Adding special effects
- Adding soundtracks
- Moving movies from iOS/iPadOS to macOS
- Using picture-in-picture
- And much more!

Are you ready to get started?!

[1]
START HERE

IMOVIE FOR…

The first thing you need to understand about iMovie is it's built for three different devices. So when I say "iMovie"—what do I mean? iMovie…for iPad? iMovie…for Mac? Or iMovie…for iPhone.

In short: yes. iMovie for all those things.

When you open iMovie on iPhone, it's going to look different than when you open it on iPad, which looks different then when you open it on Mac. But what you need to realize is, it doesn't matter. Things will be in slightly different places, but they all work essentially the same.

The focus of this book will be iPad. The reason is, it's easier to see how to do things on those bigger screens. But the logic of what you learn here can also be applied to iPhone and Mac. I'll do my best to show where things are different throughout the book.

LET'S GET STARTED!

Pick your device of choice and let's look around! On MacOS, you'll be greeted with a big welcome screen. It's much more stunning than what comes next, unfortunately.

Once you click *Continue* and get started, you get the software screen. It's pretty bare, right? That's why a lot of this book will focus on iPad—it's much easier to show you where things are on an iPad—and there are more features built into each of those. But don't worry! If you don't have an iPad, I won't leave you in the dark!

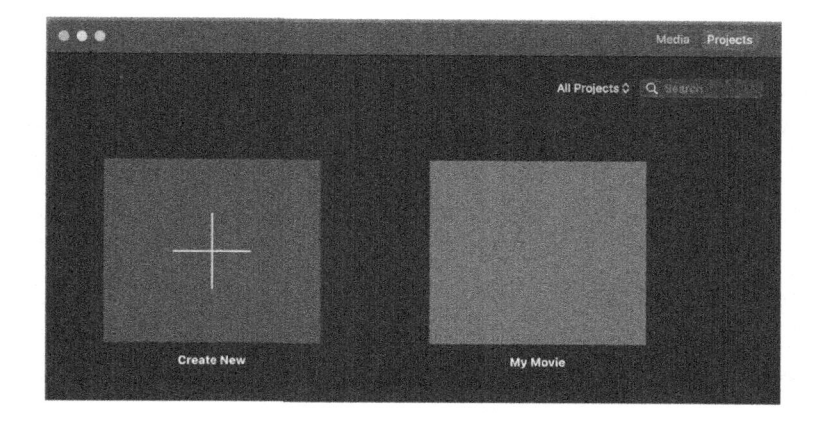

So let's look at the iPhone and iPad screens. iPhone and iPad also might feel a little…bare; there are just three options. But these options are feature-packed.

This menu is going to stay with you, but it sometimes gets minimized as it is below—if that happens, just swipe up.

The first option you'll see is *Magic Movie*. As the name implies, the movie making kind of magically happens—though there are manual changes you can make, which I'll discuss later in the book. It's going to work the same way on iPhone, but on Mac you can only edit the videos you have made on your iPad.

Storyboard lets you pick premade templates, so you can find a celebration template for, say, birthdays, as an example. As of this writing, there are 20 to pick from.

Finally, there's a start-from-scratch mode, where everything will be manual.

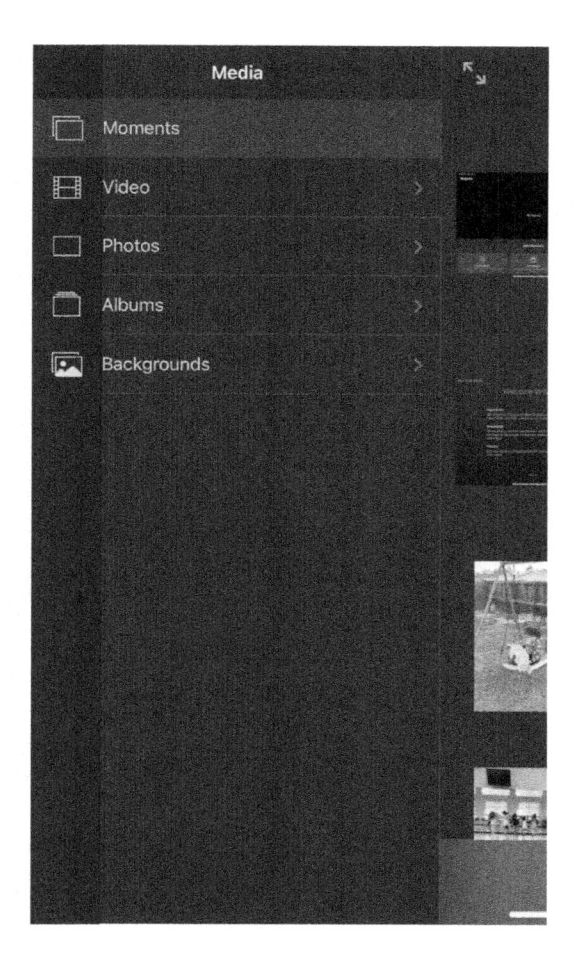

Looking at the iPhone, you should quickly see how doing these things are the same—they will just look a little different. The buttons are stacked instead of side-by-side.

Start New Project

Magic Movie
Choose your media and let iMovie create a movie for you.

Storyboard
Use beautiful templates to easily create a video or movie trailer.

Movie
Make a movie from scratch with the iMovie timeline.

[2]
Magic Movie Mode

MAGIC MOMENTS IN SECONDS

If you don't have time to get your Steven Spielberg on, and just want a video that's created effortlessly, then *Magic Moments* is the best option for you.

Magic Moments will create a themed video based on your album in just seconds.

Before you create your first magical video you need to create an album. So let's look briefly at how to do that.

CREATING AN ALBUM

You could technically add photos in one at a time, but the whole point of this powerful feature is speed: to put together a video you can share quickly. To do that, it's best to create it from an album.

There are a few things you can do. I'm going to show you the manual way first, then I'll show you a way that you might find to be a little quicker.

The manual way is to first, open the Photos app, then tap the *Select* button in the very top right corner.

From here, tap the photos you want to be in your album.

Once you select all your desired photos, go to the lower left corner, and select the square icon with the up arrow.

This will bring up a new set of options. You can either created a Shared Album or a regular album; a shared album is an album other people see. You'll notice it says, "Add to..." Kind of confusing, right? You aren't adding anything to an album—you want to create a new album. Don't worry. You'll be able to do that when you tap the *Add to Album* or *Add to Shared Album* option.

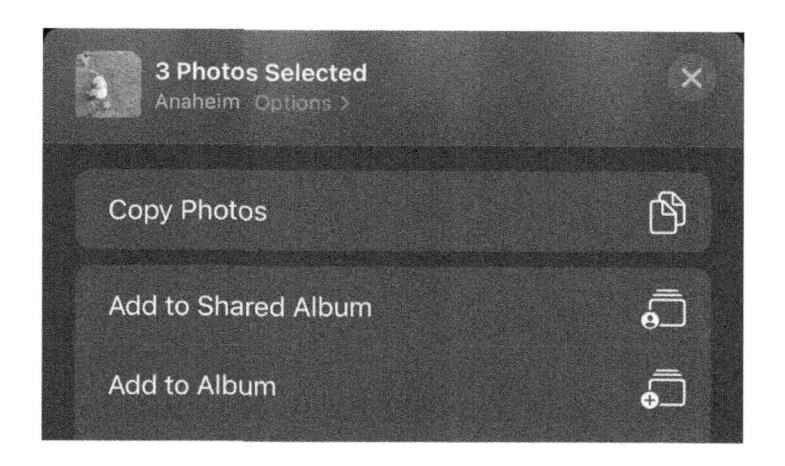

As soon as you tap *Add to Album*, look what one of the first options is: *New Album*. Tap that to create your album.

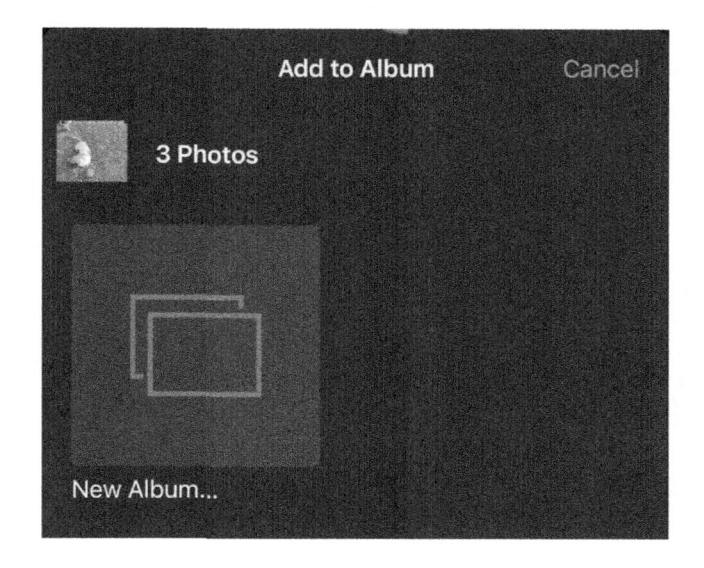

It will ask you to name your Album. Name it anything you want.

Pretty easy, right? But I said there was another way that might be a little easier. Manually creating albums is easy when you use recent photos. But what if you want to create an album about that time you went to Paris…five years ago? You don't want to scroll back five years, do you? You can quickly find it by tapping the *Search* icon in the lower right corner.

I'm going to do a search for Dog. Apple's AI is pretty smart. It can recognize when there's a dog in the photo, and it tags it as such. In the example below, it found over 400 pictures of dogs.

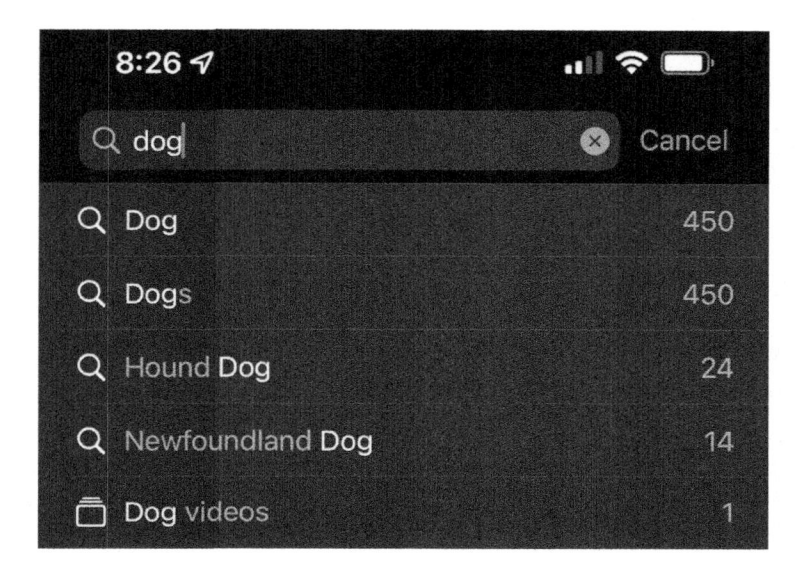

Q dog	⊗ Cancel
Q Dog	450
Q Dogs	450
Q Hound Dog	24
Q Newfoundland Dog	14
🗂 Dog videos	1

That's still a lot, but much easier to manage than manually trying to find them. You can search by people, places, animals, even objects (like flowers). From here you just repeat the steps above, selecting the photos that you want and creating your album.

Albums is where you can really start to organize things. Remember when I said above that when you press the like button on a photo it goes to the Favorites folder. This is where you'll find that folder. To add an album, tap the + button.

MAKING THE MAGICAL MOMENTS

Now that we have our albums, let's create some magical moments! Once you tap the option for *Magic Movie*, it will ask you to select the album.

It will title the video whatever your album is named. So in the example below, it's Horse Riding.

On the iPhone, the experience is exactly the same—things are just laid out differently.

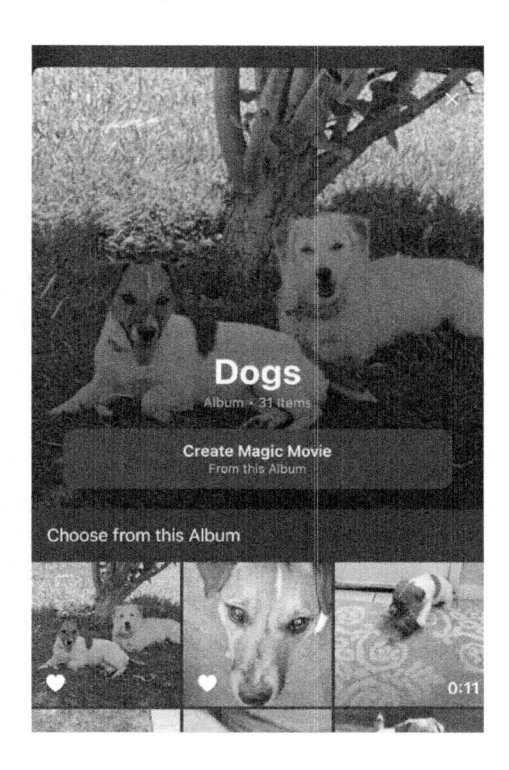

It will take a moment to generate the album. Just be patient. If these are older photos, it's probably going to be downloading them from iCloud.

Once it's created, it will come up in a video type editor.

And, again, the iPhone will be laid out differently, but all the features will work the same.

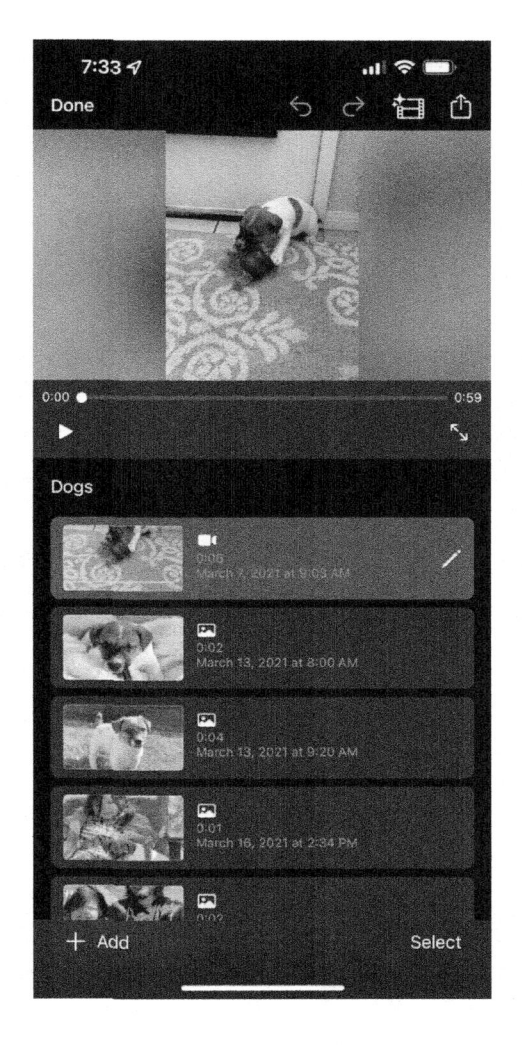

You might be working with a pretty large album. The one I'm using, for example, had over 200 images and videos (and I say images here because the movie can contain both images and videos—it can even contain just images; even if it's just images, iMovie makes them move around in a way that feels a bit like a video). iMovie hasn't included all of them. Their magical AI has decided what it thinks is the best one. As you probably know, computers are pretty smart—but they aren't perfect. And there will be some images that you might not like or you want moved. To move it, tap and hold the thumbnail and continue to hold it as you drag it to where you want it to be.

If you want to delete, change, or edit the clip, then tap the little pencil icon to the right of it. To change it, tap the *Replace* option. To edit or delete it, tap the *Edit Clip* option (yes, to delete it, you have to edit it).

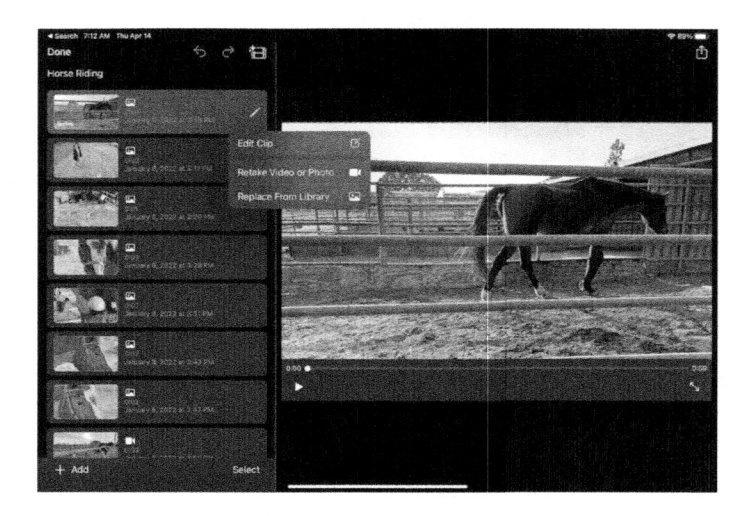

From the edit menu, you'll see lots of options. Below the image, see those yellow bars to the left and right of the clip? That lets you increase or decrease how long it shows in the video.

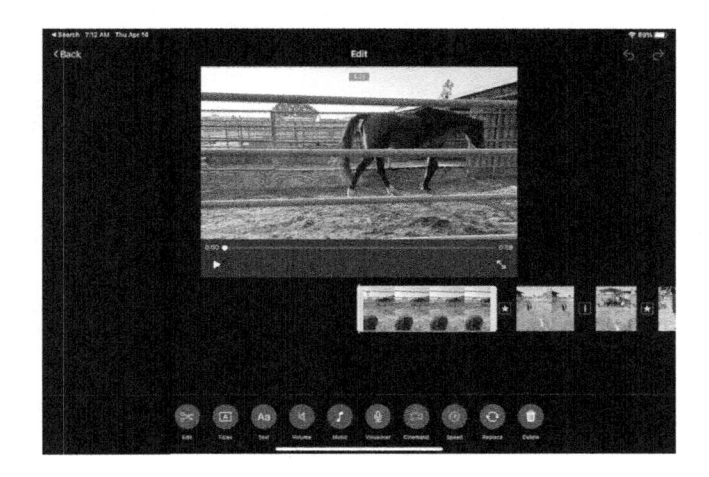

Below that, there's a row of options of different things you can add to or change in the clip. Let's look at a few of them, starting with "Titles." *Titles* lets you change the layout of the photo; there are several layouts that you can choose from.

If there's text in the clip—or you want to add in text—then use the *Text* option to add it in.

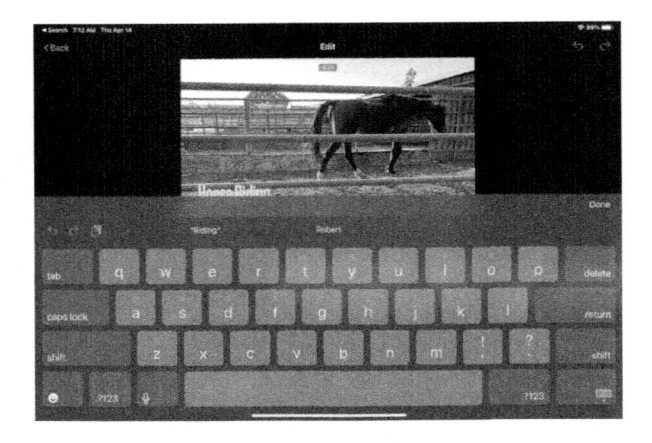

Volume lets you adjust the sound levels; meanwhile *Music*, right next to *Volume*, lets you pick the soundtrack that plays with your video (or you can take the music out); *Soundtracks* are Apple-created; below this is *My Music*, which are the songs that you have in your library. If you plan on posting this to social media (such as Facebook or YouTube), then be careful with this option—songs are licensed and having them play in the background of the video might cause the video to get removed.

The remaining options here are *Voiceover, Cinematic, Speed, Replace* and *Delete*. *Voiceover* lets you add your voice to the video; *Cinematic* only applies if you used Cinematic mode on your iPhone; *Speed* is how fast the clip moves; *Replace* lets you swap out the clip with something else; and *Delete* lets you delete the clip entirely.

When you are done, there's no need to save. Just tap the back button. Back on the main screen in the upper left corner, let's look at some more options. *Done* is what you tap when you're finished with everything; the curved left arrow is *undo* and right next to it is *redo* (it lets you undo or redo any edits you don't like). The last icon—the one with the film strip and stars—is where you change the style of the video.

There are several pre-built styles that you can use. Tap any of them to switch to it.

Underneath this, there are four options: *Music, Font, Color, Filter*. These behave like the options we just saw in the previous screens. *Music* lets you change what is playing in the movie.

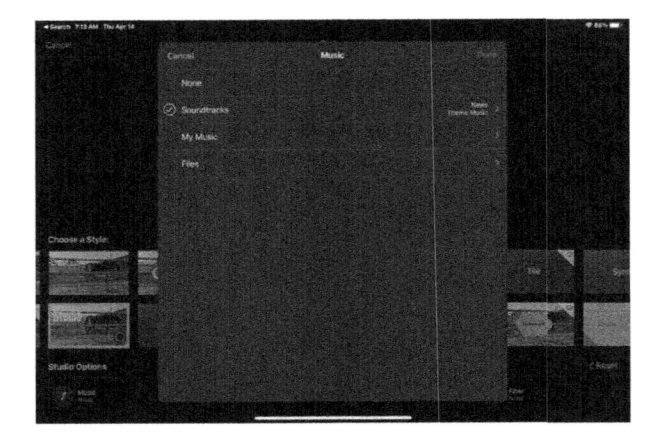

Font changes the font of the text that appears.

Color makes changes to the border colors.

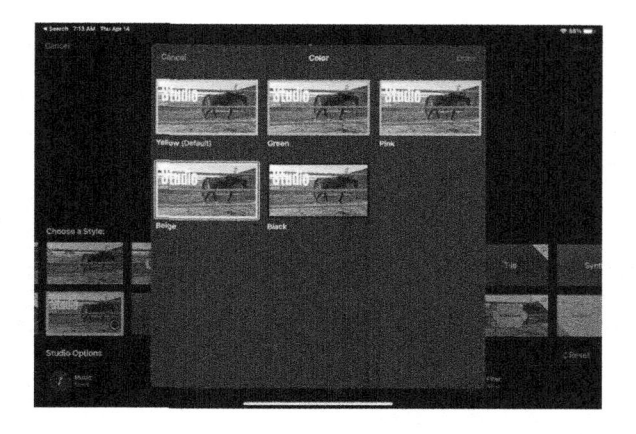

Filter lets you add a filter to your clips—make all the clips black and white, for example.

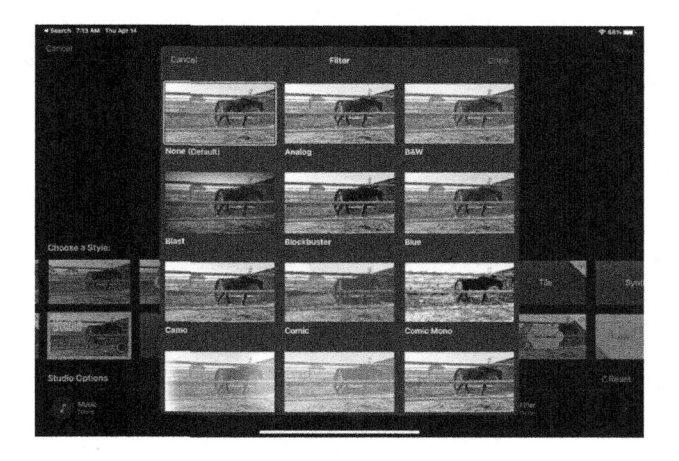

On the bottom left of the main screen, there is the option to *Add*. This lets you manually add other images or videos the AI might have missed when it put the video together.

If you want to share your amazing video, then click the square with the up arrow in the upper right corner of the main edit menu.

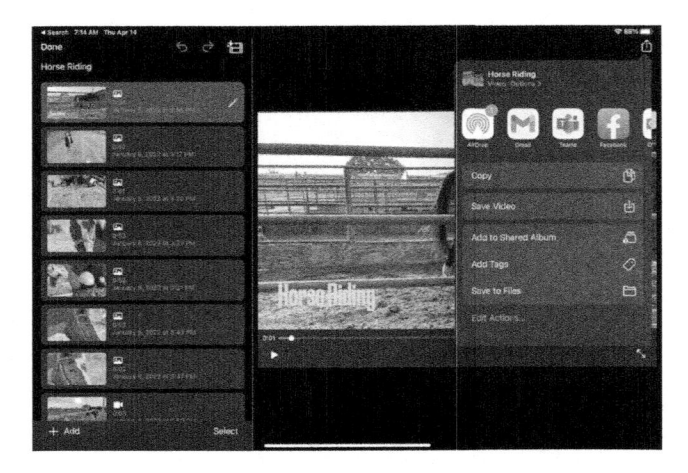

Finally, when you tap done, you'll be taken back to the main iMovie window.

If you tap on the thumbnail of the video, it will take you into the videos menu screen. From here you can edit it, play it, share it, or delete it.

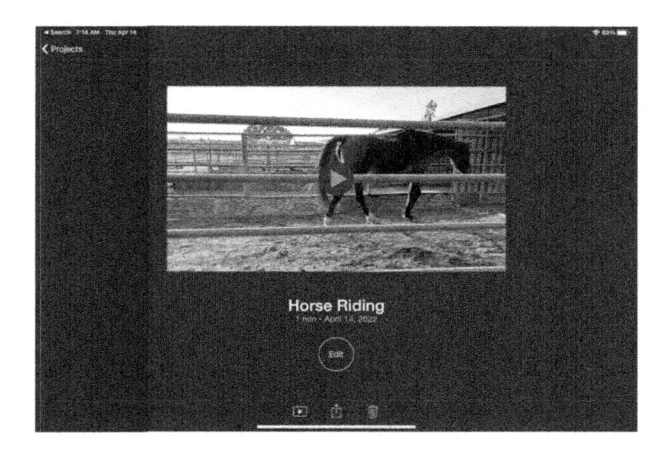

When you choose play, it will immediately go into a full screen window and play back the video for you.

SHARING AND PLAYING VIDEO

If you want to share the created video, just tap the square icon with the up arrow, then select how you want to share it. In this menu, you can also add tags to the video (these tags are searchable, which will make the video easier to find as you create several videos).

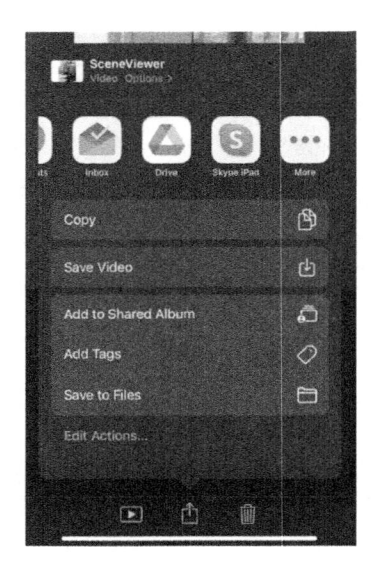

Under the video's title, you'll notice blue text that says *Options*. That's where you can change the resolution of the video—so you can make it smaller for different screens.

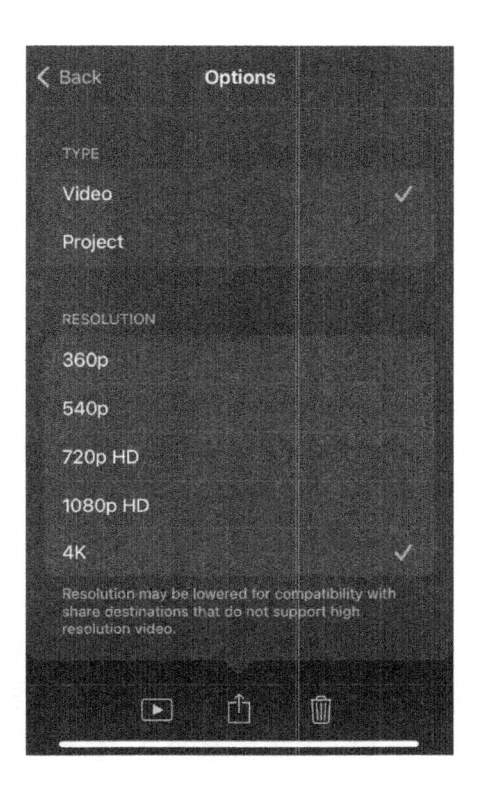

What about watching the video on a big TV? It's not obvious in these screens, but you can use AirPlay to do that. To use AirPlay, swipe down from the upper right corner to bring up the control panel.

From here, tap the two rectangle boxes that are stacked together.

This will bring up any screens you can wirelessly stream your video to. If you don't see yours, then make sure it's a compatible device (like an Apple TV) and on the same Wi-Fi network.

MOVING VIDEO FROM IPHONE / IPAD TO MAC

Now let's see how we can continue editing on your Mac; but before doing that, I'll point out quickly that this step is optional. You can do everything on your iPhone or iPad.

Like most things on the Mac, you have several ways to share it, but it all starts with the *Share* button. Before you share it, however, you need to click the *Options* button near the top of this window, then switch the type from *Video* to *Project*; if you don't do this, you'll be sharing a MOV file, which isn't the same thing as an iMovie Project file.

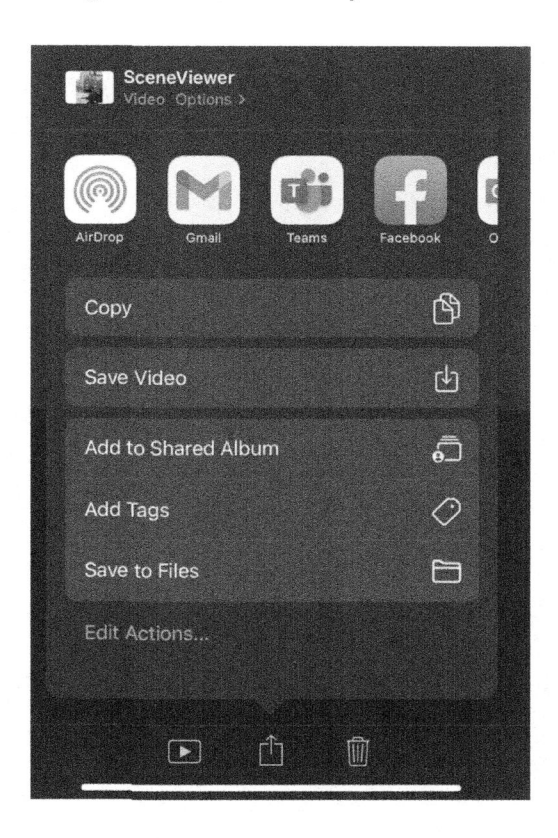

Once you make the switch, you can email it, you can plug in a USB-C device and save it to that device, or use a number of other platforms. Personally, I find the easy way to do it, however, is *AirDrop*. Assuming you are near your Mac and on the same network, you can wirelessly send it over in a matter of seconds.

If you don't see your Mac when you perform this action, it's possible that you don't have *AirDrop* turned on or set up correctly. Click the *Control Panel* in the upper right corner of your Mac (it's to the left of the *Siri* button). *AirDrop* should be blue. If it says *Contacts Only*, you can click on it and set it to *Everyone* to see if this fixes the problem. Once it's sent over, you'll find it in the Downloads section of Finder.

Once you find the file and open it, it will launch iMovie, where you can start making changes. Don't worry about how to make those changes…yet. I'll cover that in the last chapter.

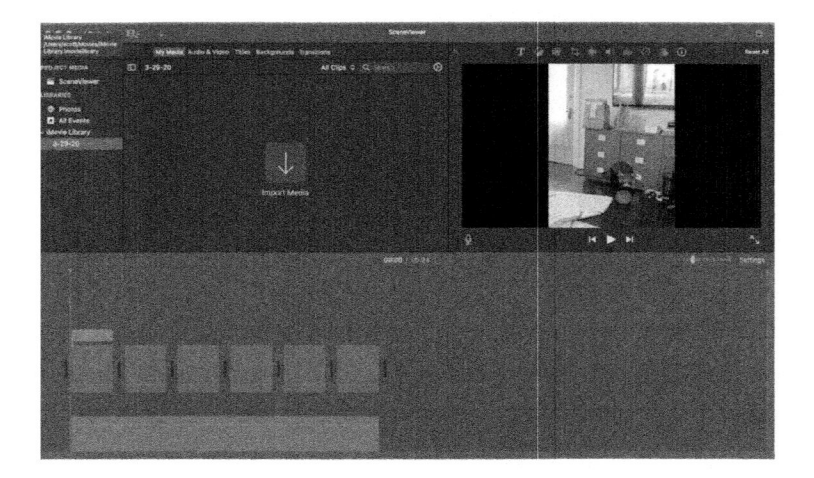

[3]
STORYBOARDS MODE

Years ago, when iMovie was first released on iOS, I remember they had this really cool thing to create movie trailers with your home movies. You picked what you wanted to make—an action trailer, a romance, a thriller, etc. Then it would say things like "find a 30 second video with two people walking." At the end of it, you'd have this fun movie trailer you could share with families.

This mode is still there, but Apple has revamped it. Instead of just creating movie trailers, you can create a bunch of other things. If you want to create a DIY video, for example, there's a template for that. It will plug in a template and you just fill in the blanks.

This is what Storyboards mode is all about.

As of this writing, there are over 20 templates to pick from:

- About Me
- Celebration
- Cooking
- Day in the Life
- DIY
- Gaming
- How It Works
- Makeover
- Q&A
- Film
- Thank You
- Top 5
- Trip
- Wellness
- Product Pitch
- Product Review
- Reveal
- Book Report
- News Report
- Science Experiment
- Trailers

Now all of them are on your iPhone or iPad—that's what the little cloud icons in the upper right corner mean; if you are using iMovie where you might not have Internet, then you can go to the bottom and select *Download All*.

Once you pick out what template to use, you'll need to start customizing it. Again, you'll notice here that some elements need to be downloaded. This is just to save on storage, but they're very quick downloads. Just keep it in mind if you will be working on this project without Internet.

And remember, the iPhone works the same way; things are just laid out slightly differently; but if you know how to use iMovie on the iPad, then you know how to use it on the iPhone.

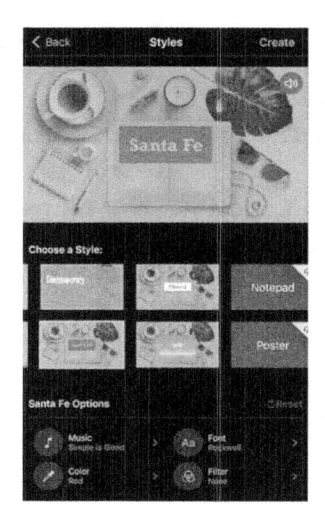

After you make all the adjustments that you want to make, tap *Create* in the upper right corner. Now, let's look at some of the adjustments you can make. *Styles* is the most obvious choice; this is the overall look of your video—the types of backgrounds that will appear on the title, for example. Scroll down and there are more options. The first is *Music*. This works just like it did for Magic Movie; you can use the default soundtrack that Apple suggests, choose something different in *Soundtracks*, or look through your music to find a song in your library. *Soundtracks* is created by Apple; *My Music* is songs that you own.

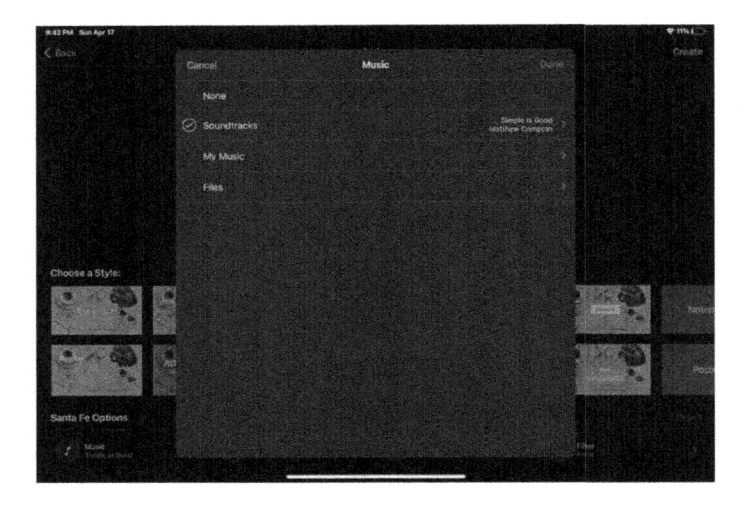

Next to music is *Color*. As the name suggests, the *Color* option lets you pick the background colors that appear in your video.

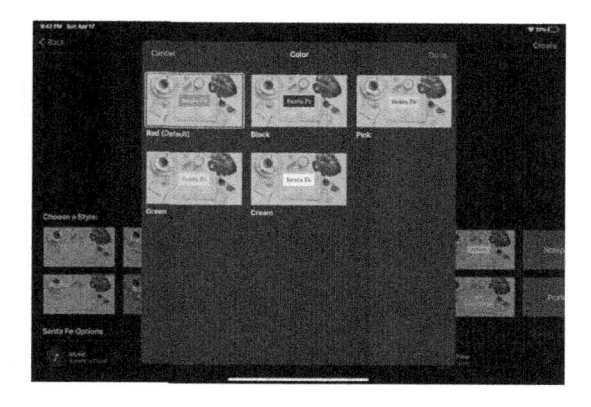

The *Fonts* option lets you pick the best font for your video.

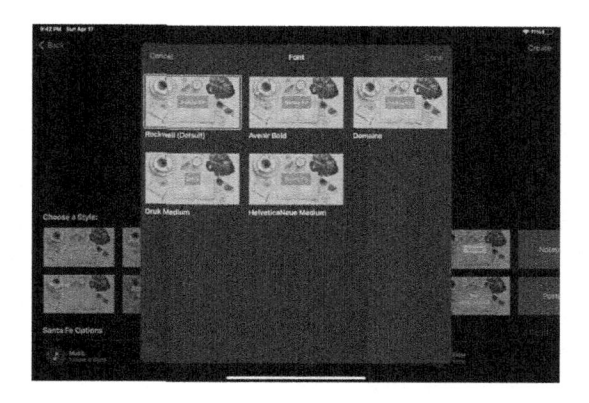

Finally, the *Filter* option lets you add filters to your video—you can make it look black and white, for example, or give it a saturated hue.

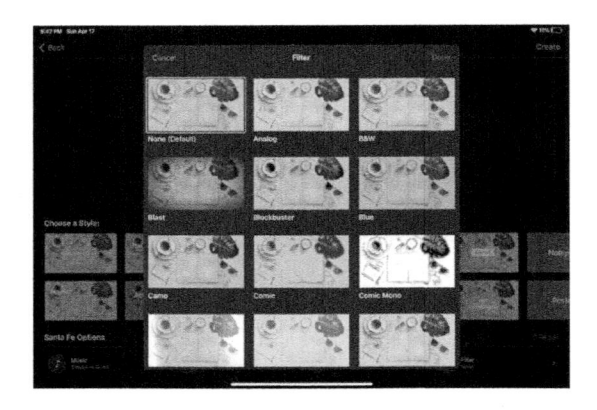

Once you have added your desired customizations, tap *Create* in the upper right corner.

You will now be brought into the main editor. As the name implies, this interface is meant to resemble a Storyboard in a movie production. So it gives you kind of a script—notice each section has a name (i.e. Who, What, Experience, etc)? These are meant to be the themes of each section; in *Who*, for example, you would find a video with yourself explaining who you are—the template I picked was "About Me" which is a mini bio video; if I had picked something else (like Gaming, DIY, Makeover, etc.) it would have listed different Storyboards. In each section it will tell you what kind of shot you should have; for example, the one in the example below says to make the first shot a Medium Shot—meaning not from a distance and not closeup—it also gives a preview of a person meant to represent approximately where the shot should be.

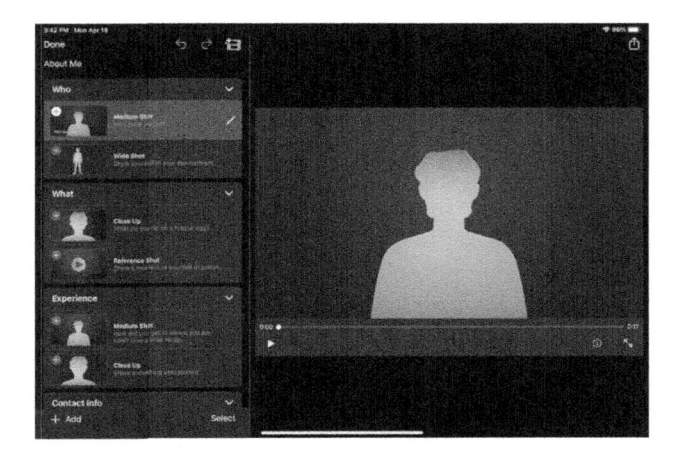

You can tap the arrow icons on the right to collapse or expand any section.

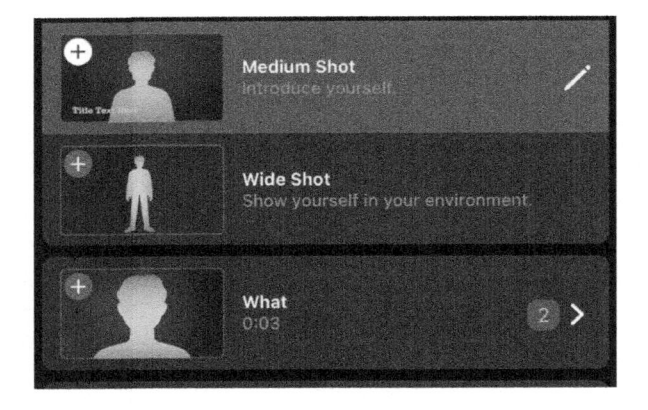

You can also tap *Add* in the lower left corner to manually add a video or clip that's not in the Storyboard.

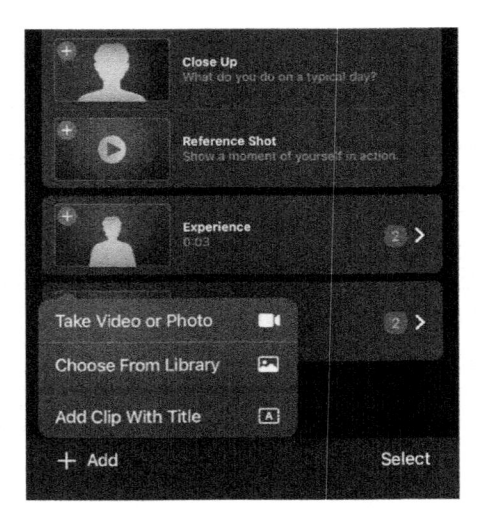

To add a video to the Storyboard, click the + icon in the thumbnail image.

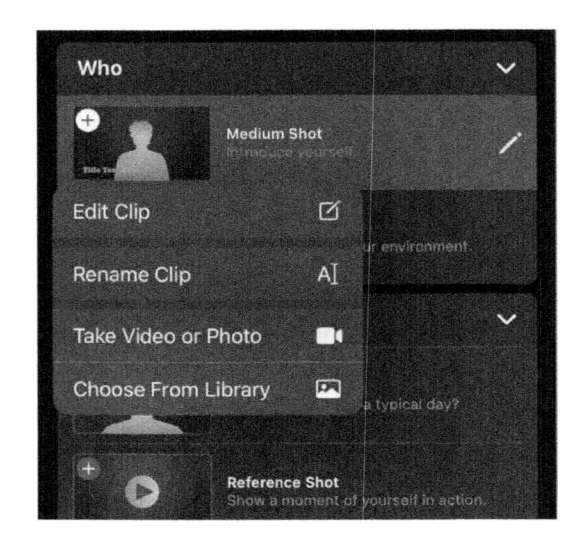

You can also do this by tapping on the pencil icon to the right. In this same menu, you can rename the clip; so, for example, if you don't like "Medium Shot," you can rename it to something that suits it better—this title is just for informative purposes while editing—it does not show up in the video when it is done.

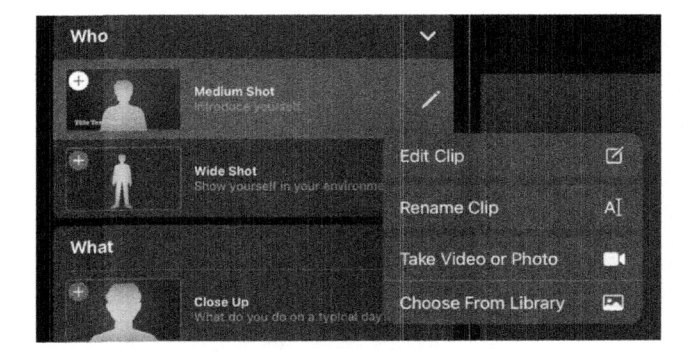

When you tap the ⓘ icon on the preview, it will show you the title of the shot that's currently playing in the preview.

If you made a mistake, you can use the *undo* button up on top; you can also use that video with the stars icon to change the formatting around. If you decide to use a different font / style or want to swap the music out, tap on this.

To share the video, tap on the share icon in the upper right corner. Remember, the *Options* button near the top lets you toggle between sharing a project or a MOV file.

MOV can be viewed on most devices (including non-Apple devices); project files require iMovie to open.

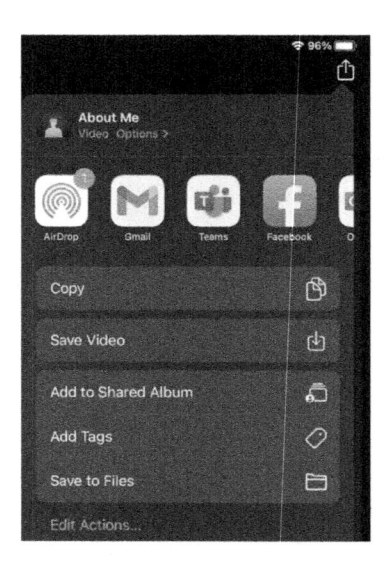

EDITING A STORYBOARD

Storyboards are pretty straightforward, right? Just add the video or image and you're done? Kind of. But that's not always the case. Sometimes you want to have text on the clip; sometimes you want the clip to appear longer or shorter; sometimes you want voiceover; sometimes…you get the idea? There are time that you might not want to settle for everything in the template.

In cases where you want to make tweaks, add in your clip as you normally would, then tap *Preview* and then *Edit Clip*.

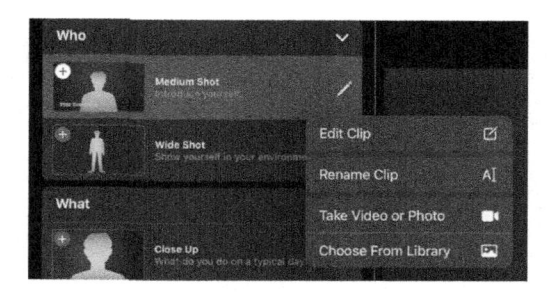

This brings up the edit screen with lots of extra features. You'll notice that you can edit the entire series of clips here—you don't just edit one clip; the entire video shows up.

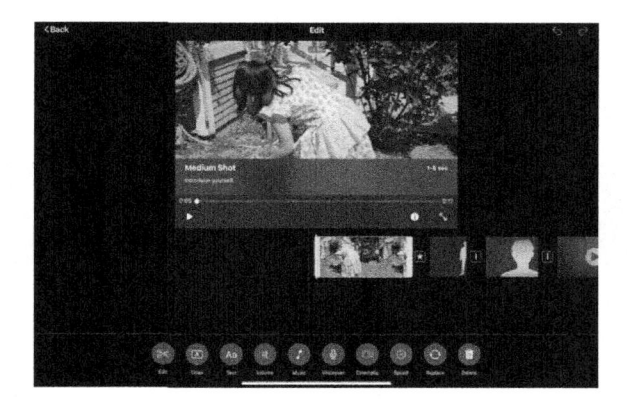

One of the most common changes you'll make is how long a clip is. Each clip has a yellow box around it with two thick yellow edges. Those edges can be dragged in and out—so, for example, if you want to edit the beginning of the clip, you would drag the yellow edge on the left inward or outward; if it's at the end of the clip, then you use the right edge.

On the bottom is a list of options you can add to each clip. Emphasis on the word "clip." You are *only* making changes to each selected clip, not the entire video. So tapping on *Text* will not add text to the entire video—just the selected clip.

[4]
MAKE A MOVIE FROM SCRATCH

Magic Movie Mode and Storyboards Mode are great…but sometimes you want full control of your video. For that, there's Manual Mode. Let's get ready to get our Spielberg on and figure out how it works.

Here's the good news: now that you've come this far, Manual Mode really won't seem that hard. Many of the features work the same; the only difference is it's not quite as guided. You must let your creativity take over and do everything yourself.

The first thing you'll see is a big gallery to pick what you want the movie to include. You'll see Moments (which are things generated based on what your phone thinks are important), Videos, Photos, Albums and Backgrounds. If you don't know what you'll include, then you can select *Create Movie* near the bottom middle of the screen and create it with no videos.

Backgrounds kind of sounds like backgrounds you've downloaded onto your device. It's not. It's actually just background color choices.

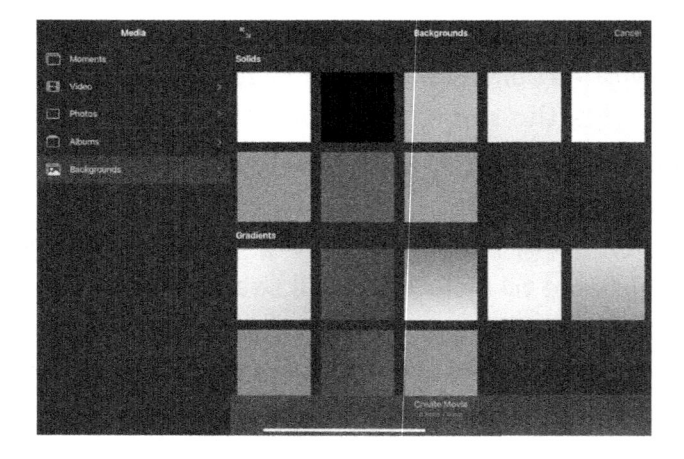

Once you select *Create Movie*, you'll either see the clip you initially selected or a blank preview. From here you can start editing the clip or adding new ones. To add a new one, go to the right menu area where it says *Media*. You find your content the same way as before—and remember you can pick movies or photos.

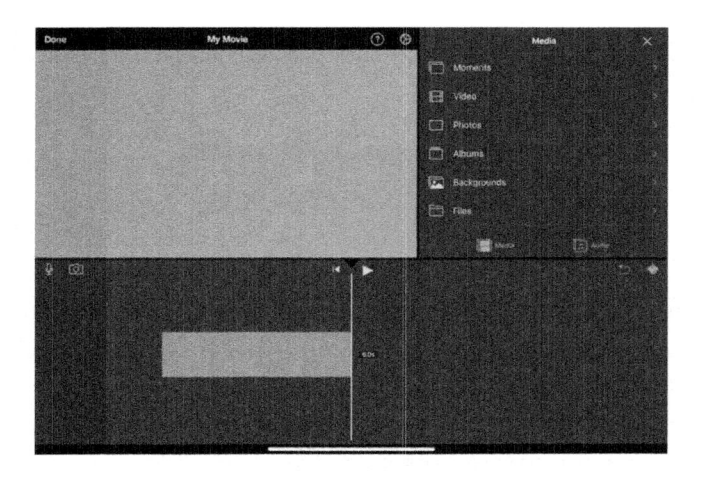

To save on space, many people choose to store videos and photos automatically onto iCloud. This lets you create large videos and not have to worry about not having enough room. When you do this, however, you'll have to redownload them to use them. You'll know if your content is on your device or in the cloud by the icon when you click it. In the example below, I can play it, but I cannot add it to iMovie because it's in the cloud. To download it, I would only need to tap that cloud with the down arrow. How does it show it if it's in the cloud? A small preview is stored on your phone and you can stream it from the cloud.

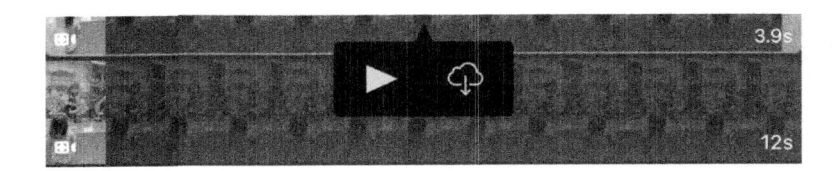

As soon as I tap that cloud, then it's on my device after it downloads, and the cloud changes to a + icon, which indicates it can be added to the movie. To add it, just tap the + icon.

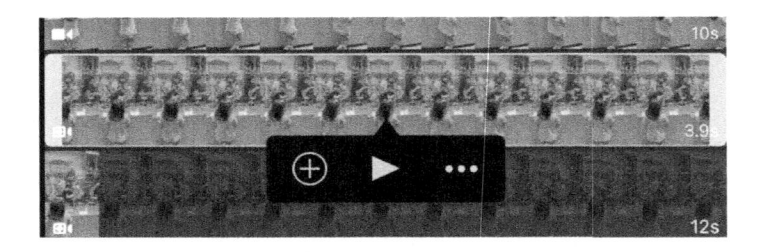

When you tap the + icon, it will add it behind the last clip—you can tap and hold any clip to drag its placement around.

Once the clip is added in, click on it to see options available to that clip. There are five:
- **Actions** – This lets you trim / crop a clip.
- **Speed** – Let's you adjust the timing of the clip—so it could have the same amount of content, but it appears for more or less time.
- **Volume** – Adjusts how loud or soft music in the background plays.
- **Titles** – You can add or adjust any text in the clip here.

- **Filters** – Adjust the overall style / look of the clip with this action.

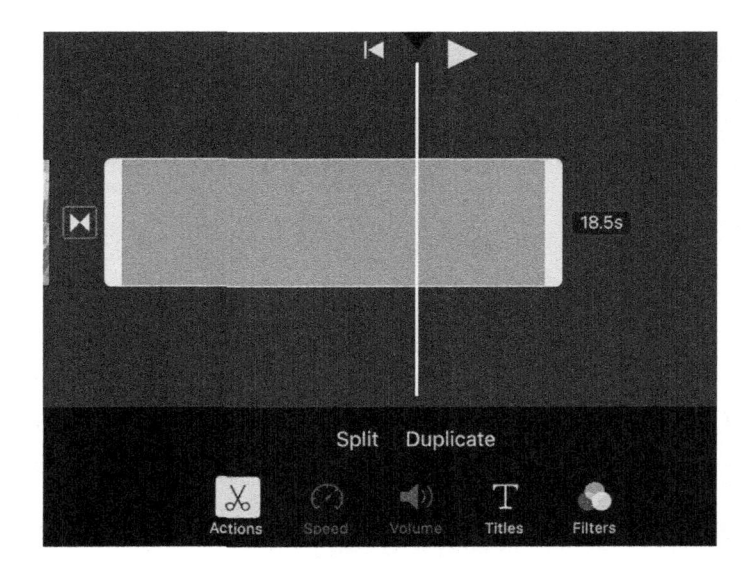

Manual Controls

Let's take a quick look at some of the manual icons that you'll see—there aren't many of them.

Under the main video preview, there are four icons. Starting on the left, the first, the microphone, lets you add voiceover narration to a clip; the next is the camera, which lets you take a video or picture that you'll add into the video; on the right, the back arrow with the line jumps to the previous clip; and finally, the forward arrow plays a preview of the video.

Over on the far right, there's an undo button, which reverses any changes you might have made by mistake; next to *undo* is the *audio reveal*; when you tap that, it will show any audio that is in the clip.

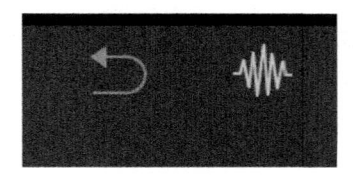

In the example below, you can see the first clip has a little bit of soft audio playing in the background; this helps me know if there might be something in the clip that I want to mute or amplify.

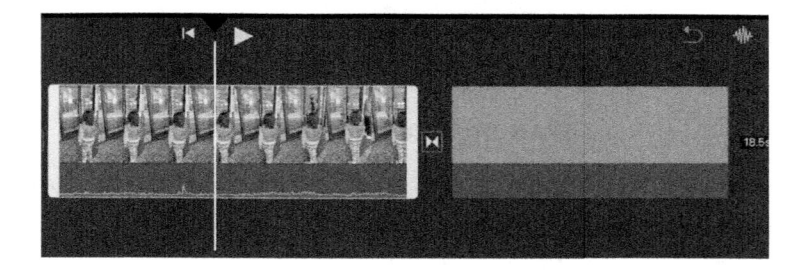

On the top, near the middle of the main screen is a config icon. This lets you add filters, change the main theme, and toggle on and off music and transitions.

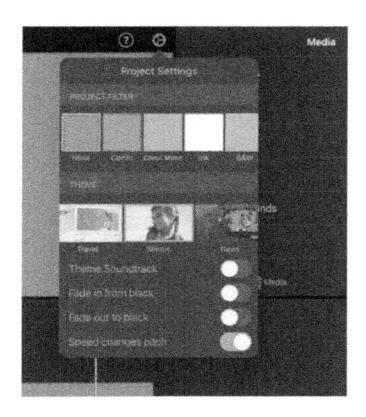

ADDING TRANSITIONS

If you want to add a transition between clips, then tap the two arrows facing each other in the middle of two clips; this will reveal transition options. Tap the one you want. You can also adjust how long you want the transition to take (1.0 seconds is the default).

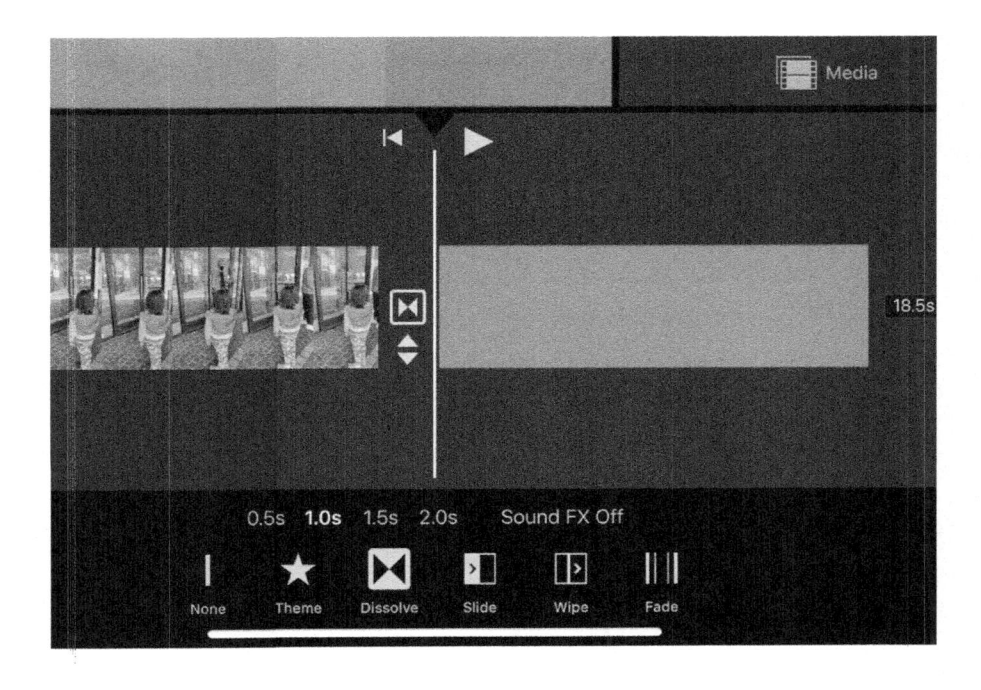

[5]
iMovie For MacOS

For the power user inside you, you'll want to head to iMovie for MacOS to get the most out of iMovie.

Opening it for the first time can be a little intimidating; unlike iOS and iPadOS, the controls and where they are look nothing like what we've seen thus far. Don't let the fresh look scare you—once you get used to it, it really does behave in a similar way.

Before continuing further, let me say once more: you do not need MacOS to make a good movie; iOS and iPadOS can deliver superior results. The main reason you might consider using MacOS over a mobile device is it works more like a film editor and some users will prefer this format.

So let's get started!

Downloading iMovie

iMovie should be preinstalled on your Mac; you'll find the icon in your launchpad.

If you don't see it, then it's possible you might have removed it on accident.

To get a new copy, just go into the App store, search for iMovie, and click *Get*. It's free, but it is large, so it might take some time to download.

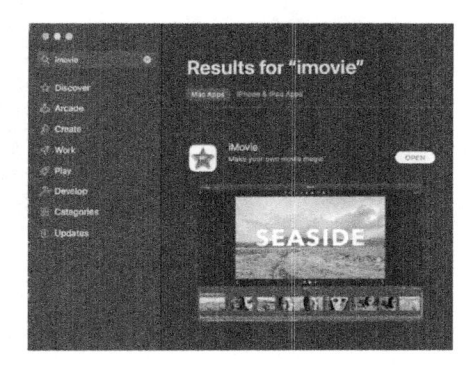

STARTING A NEW PROJECT

When you first start iMovie, it's probably going to feel a little…lacking. It literally has one option: *Create New*.

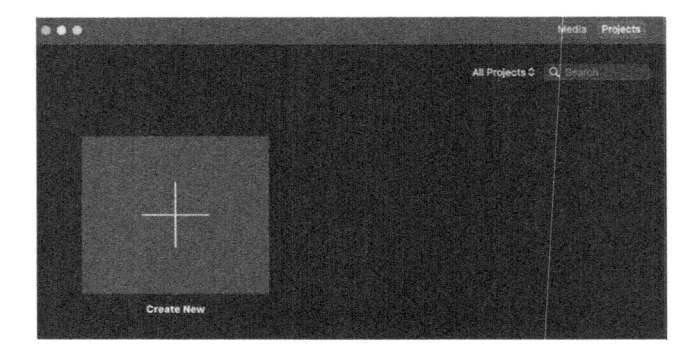

When you click on *Create New*, you'll get another option: *Movie* and *Trailer*.

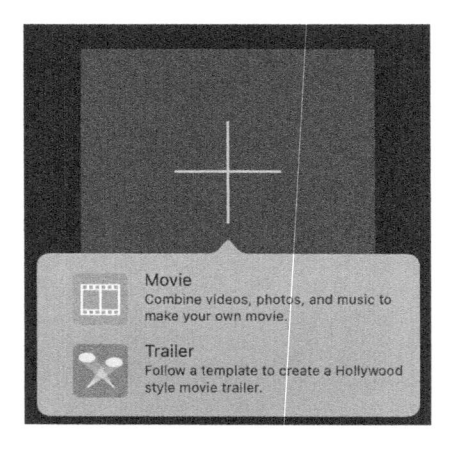

At some point, I suspect Apple will add in the same options as iOS and iPadOS, but, as of this writing, that is not the case. So all we get is *Trailer*, which is very similar to *Storyboard* on mobile devices.

When you click *Trailer*, you'll see all kinds of different styles that are available to you. Like they do on mobile devices, these create mini movies—about a minute and a half in length; they feel cinematic—like a movie trailer. They're fun to try out, but not quite as powerful as the Storyboard mode available on iOS and iPadOS.

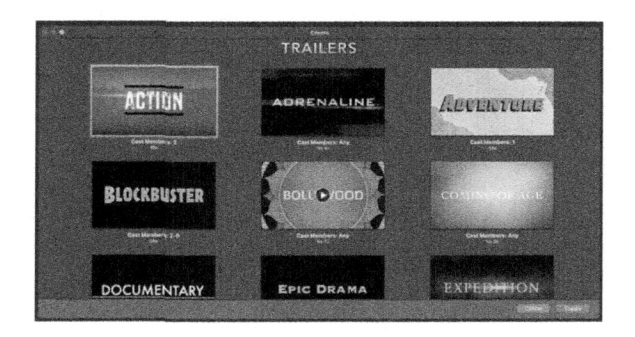

When you use this mode, you'll see that the options are also pretty similar to mobile devices. Click on *Storyboard* and drag in the content that you want.

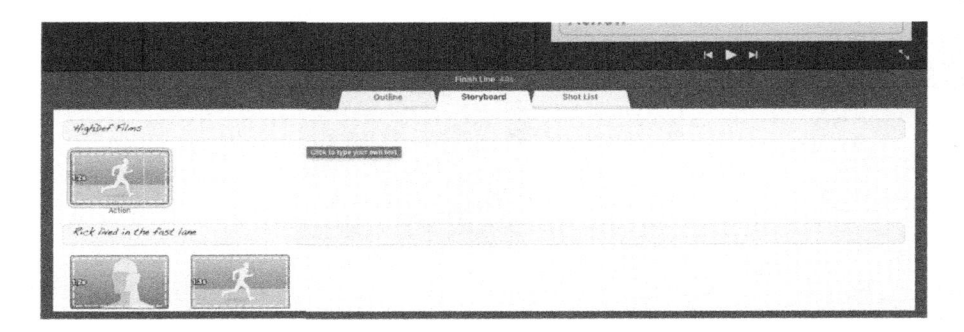

CREATING YOUR FIRST MOVIE

When you create a movie, the first thing you'll see is a blank canvas.

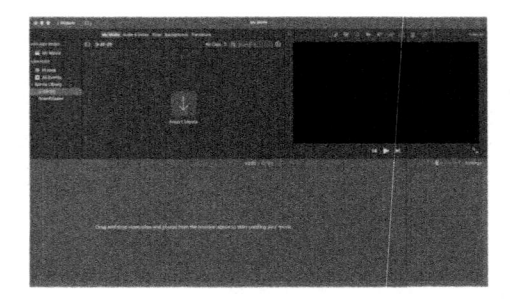

So your first step is really to start adding some (or all) of your content.

There are a few ways to add in your content; you can click *Import Media* and find it.

You can go into the search menu and look for it.

You can look for it in the left media menu.

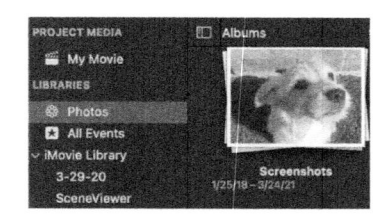

Or, perhaps the easiest—certainly my preferred method—you can drag and drop it in.

CREATING TITLE, BACKGROUNDS, TRANSITIONS, AND MORE

You may have noticed a menu on top that says: My Media, Audio & Video, Titles, Backgrounds, Transitions. This is always available to you. So any time you want to add a transition or music or titles, then go to this menu.

My Media   Audio & Video   Titles   Backgrounds   Transitions

To add in the effect, find what you want and then drag it into the film editor in the bottom half of the screen.

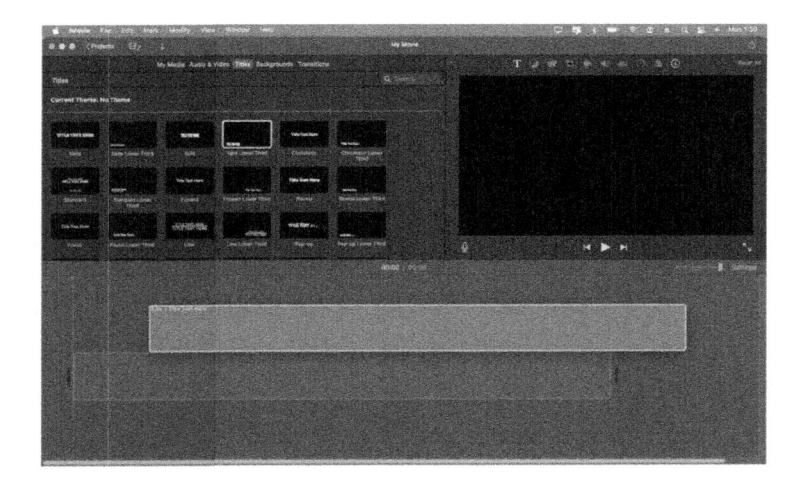

MANAGING THE FILM EDITOR

The area you'll spend the most time is the editor that covers the bottom half of your screen.

The film editor has several different rows that each serve as a layer. You'll have a row for the video / photo, one for text, one for audio—you might have several rows for each. If you are familiar with photo editors, then this concept of layers might be familiar to you. The idea is each row is stacked on top of each other and you can edit each row independently. So if you needed one text to be more transparent than another, then you would be able to do that.

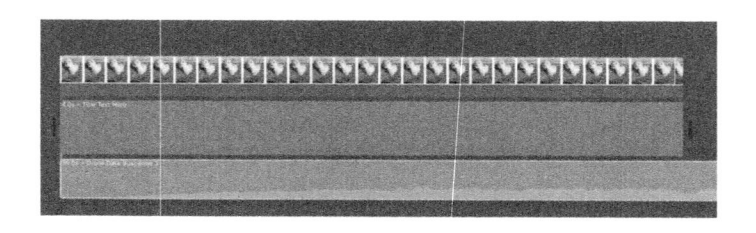

If rows and layers are still a little confusing, then hang in there. As you understand the controls better, it will start making more sense.

Editing Clips

Videos, text, and audio each have different options you can use. So as you click on different clips in the editor, you'll notice that the menu options in the upper right half are changing based on what you are clicking on. Many of these controls will be familiar to you from the mobile versions of the app. I'll briefly address each option and go over differences—if any.

Starting on the far left, the *Magic Wizard* icon doesn't bring up any menus; it works in the background to automatically perfect the image or video; it will make automatic color adjustments.

The next set of options is the video overlay. These are affects you can use to make the video or text more transparent (opacity). So if you have text appearing on top of the video, and you find it isn't showing correctly, then you can use *Opacity* and *Fade* to adjust the video and make the text easier to read.

The dropdown says *Cutaway* by default, but if you click on it, you'll see there are several other options. *Green / Blue Screen* for example, attempts to remove the background.

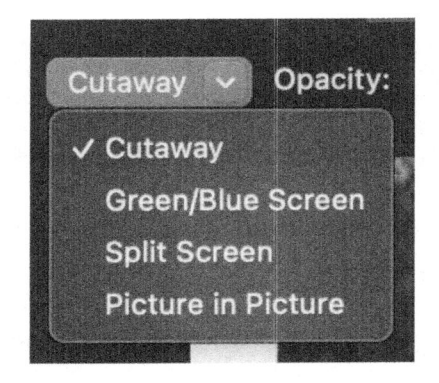

Picture in Picture minimizes the video clip and puts it in the corner of the screen. This technique works well with instructional videos where you are showing the teacher in the corner box, and the illustration in the main area. As you adjust these settings, you'll also notice the menu slightly changes to have additional options.

Color Balance is the next icon; you can use *Auto* to make auto adjustments to the color, or use some of the manual adjustments.

Color Corrections is next; it lets you adjust the hue and contrasts of the colors.

Cropping is the fourth icon and one you will want to pay particular attention to if you are using photos. By default, photos will take the Ken Burns effect; what's that? That means the image is zoomed to a certain section and as the movie plays it moves over other areas—to give the impression that the photo is a movie of sorts. *Crop to Fill* and *Fit* might look better for some photos. To the right of these options are buttons to rotate the photo.

Got a shaky hand? Me too! *Stabilization* can help you with that. It's going to prove especially helpful if you took action shots.

Volume lets you adjust how loud a clip is—you can lower it so other clips running alongside it are louder. For example, you might have a music track and only want to be able to slightly hear the sound in the video.

Noise Reduction and *Equalizer* help you adjust the volume even more; let's say you shot the video in a crowded restaurant or somewhere with lots of racket. This option can help correct some of that background noise.

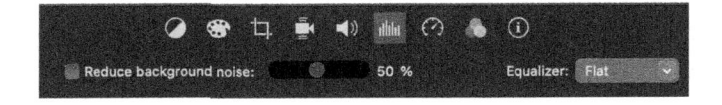

To the right of these tools is a dropdown that says *Equalizer*. There are several more enhancements when you click on that.

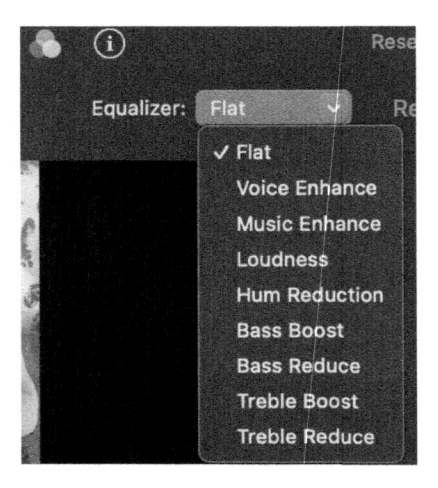

Speed adjusts not only how fast the video plays, but can also play the clip in reverse.

Clip Filter and *Audio Effects* include both visual and audio enhancements to the clip.

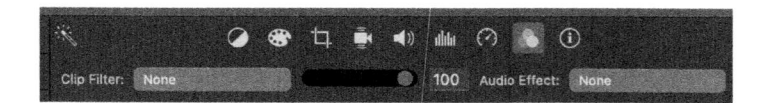

Clip Information is the last option; this will tell you information about when the video was taken and how long it is.

EDITING A CLIP

When you right-click a clip, you'll be shown several options; some (i.e. Play, Cut, Copy, and Delete) will be familiar to you and not need explaining; the rest might be a little confusing, so let's look at each.

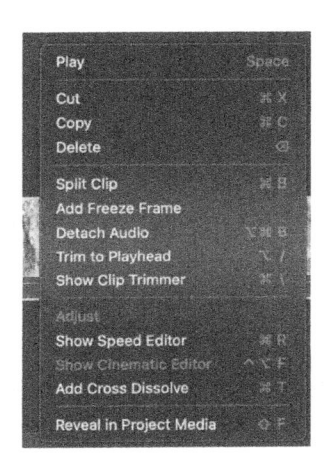

- *Split Clip* – Splitting a clip means you are cutting the clip—that lets you do independent edits to the video; it's useful if you want to have audio playing for only part of the video, for example. To split the clip, move to the part of the clip you want to separate, then right-click and select *split*.
- *Add Freeze Frame* – *Freeze Frame* will freeze the video for a specified amount of time, and then start playing it again.
- *Detach Audio* – By default, the video's audio is attached to the video itself—that means you edit the audio alongside the video. Detaching it will separate the audio from the video and it will show on a separate row of the editor.

- *Trim to Playhead* – *Trim to Playhead* is basically cropping. You move the cursor to where you want to crop, then right-click and select this option; it will crop to that point in the clip.
- *Show Clip Trimmer* – *Clip Trimmer* is another cropping tool that helps you hone in on the precise moment you want to trim.
- *Show Speed Editor* – *Speed Editor* might appear to do nothing at first; the editor is actually above the preview in the upper right corner and is also available when you click the associated icon.
- *Show Cinematic Editor* – Most of your videos probably won't show this; Cinematic mode was added to the newest iPhones (it's the mode that blurs things in a video that are not the focus—it's like portrait mode, but with video). If you didn't shoot the video in Cinematic mode, this option will be disabled.
- *Add Cross Dissolve* – A cross dissolve lets you gently increase the opacity of one scene over the previous one.
- *Reveal in Project Media* – This option shows the location of the file in the project media (the box that shows all media that's contained inside a project).

ADD A VOICEOVER

To add a voiceover to a movie, you'll go to a somewhat unusual place: the top of iMovie. Click the *Window* menu, then select *Record Voiceover*.

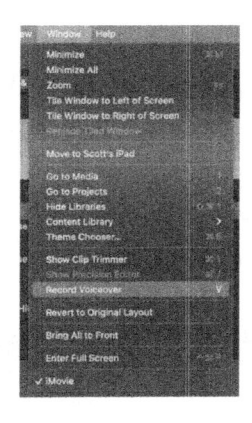

This will put a record button under the preview of your video; click record to add the voiceover.

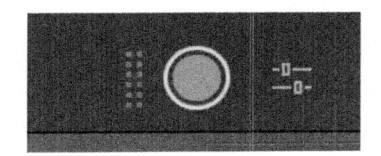

ADD A THEME

Okay, so remember when I said iMovie for Mac doesn't have all those fancy templates. That's true. But they do have *some* templates. They're called themes. You can access them in the same menu as *Voiceover Windows > Theme Chooser*.

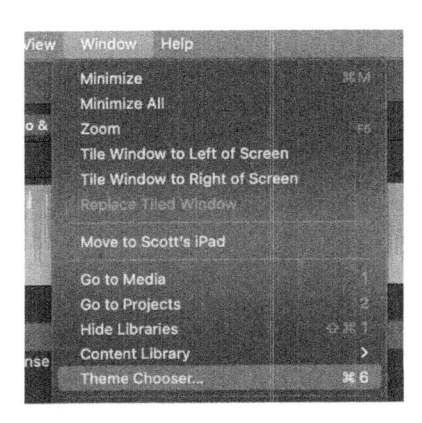

This will bring up several Themes that you can pick from. It's not quite as robust as the mobile versions of the app, but it's a nice way to get started on a project. You can preview each one, and if you want to add one, then click the *Change* button on the lower right corner.

SAVING / SHARING MOVIE

When you are done with a project, there's no "Save" button; you save by clicking on the *<Project* button in the upper left corner. It will ask you what you want to name it, then return you to the main screen.

If you want to share it, then go to *File > Share* and select how you want to share it.

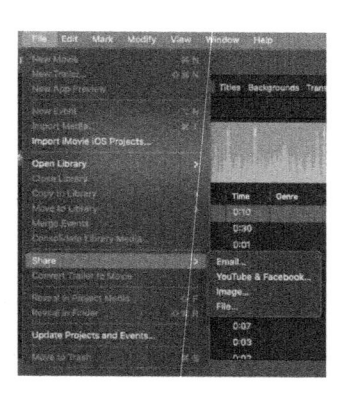

INDEX

A

Album 13, 14, 15
Audio Effect 64

B

Backgrounds 47, 48, 59

C

Color 25, 26, 38, 62
Color Balance 62
Color Correction 62
Crop 62

D

Detach Audio 65
Downloading 54

E

Editing 44, 60, 65
Equalizer 63

F

Film Editor 59

I

Internet 2

K

Ken Burns 62

M

Magic Moments 13

Moving 32
Music 25, 38

N

Noise Reduction 63

O

Opacity 61

P

Photo Albums 18
Photos 13, 47
Picture in Picture 61
Playing 30

S

Sharing 30, 68
Split 65
Stabilization 63
Storyboard 10, 40, 41, 42, 44, 56, 57

T

Theme 67
Titles 23, 50, 59
Trailer 56
Transitions 53, 59
Trim 66

V

Voiceover 24, 66, 67

ABOUT THE AUTHOR

Scott La Counte is a librarian and writer. His first book, *Quiet, Please: Dispatches from a Public Librarian* (Da Capo 2008) was the editor's choice for the Chicago Tribune and a Discovery title for the Los Angeles Times; in 2011, he published the YA book The N00b Warriors, which became a #1 Amazon bestseller; his most recent book is *#OrganicJesus: Finding Your Way to an Unprocessed, GMO-Free Christianity* (Kregel 2016).

He has written dozens of best-selling how-to guides on tech products.

You can connect with him at ScottDouglas.org.

Printed in Great Britain
by Amazon